THE RESILIENT WOMAN

How To Succeed In A World That Is Against You

JANET BRYAN

TABLE OF CONTENTS

INTRODUCTION

It is easy to accept whatever comes your way and give up your hopes and aspirations in this world full of biases and preconceptions, particularly towards women. It is simpler to merely be a man's fantasy; all you have to do is sit back and appear in their imagination, then one day you may become a housewife, cheerleader, housekeeper, or anything else but what you want to do with your life. Because it is simpler to go with the flow, you give up on your goals, extinguish your enthusiasm, and settle. You wind up being sad and unsatisfied even though you could be living a better life.

Stereotypes are ubiquitous, widely-held ideas that influence how we perceive our skills and those of others. They are outright lies or possibly half-truths that are propagated by the general public to keep you in a chokehold and dissuade you from realizing all of your potential once you buy into these specific concepts. By influencing your aspirations,

sources of support, opportunities, access to resources, and perceptions, gender stereotypes have a significant impact on you, navigating your life and career. This is a significant obstacle
to the advancement of women in critical areas, such as management. the

continued low involvement and representation of women

in positions of high management.

Until these stereotypes are changed, it's essential to think about how to better inoculate oneself from biases induced by stereotypes, helping you to pursue fulfilling careers in the areas where your passions and talents lie.

CHAPTER ONE

DARE TO DREAM

Being dismantled by the power of stereotypes, your wings get clipped and you become your weakest version, not being able to soar. You opt for the very least since it's the norm,

instead of chasing 'shadows'. These 'shadows' were once what made you happy and lit the spark in your heart, giving you hope and something to look forward to. How then did your dreams become mere shadows, if not because you bought into those self-limiting stereotypes? The good thing is you can change this. You can still dream again.

Reigniting passion

You change this reality you are in, only by changing your mindset first. Know the ways these stereotypes influence you, so you don't think the choices you made, before this moment, that led you here were purely your decisions.

Here's how;

Become Aware

Learn more about how gender stereotypes affect several aspects of your life, such as entrepreneurship, economic engagement, the division of unpaid caregiving, and empowerment.

Know how gender stereotypes affect the realization of rights and

equitable opportunities, including those relating to economic participation and entrepreneurship.

Take Action

Take specific action to stop and eradicate gender stereotypes and the detrimental effects they have

in both the public and private realms.

The first step is to get rid of the stereotypical mentality and make good mental notes like; *"I am more than a mother, wife, girlfriend, or daughter—these are only labels indicating relationship — I can be* more "

To dismantle gender stereotypes and advance gender equality, also engage in advocacy and campaigning with others.

You have aspirations and desires, run with them. Do not

let social expectations derail your childhood aspirations! You may be more if you want to, but becoming more

requires effort, growth-oriented learning, sustained passion, and a refusal to accept anything less.

CHAPTER TWO

NO LIMITS

Thriving is a mandate, you should soar even. Whatever dream you have is valid and not in any way overboard.

You need to get your mind right, and your steps on point.

It starts with you. You have made a lot of compromises and chosen to sacrifice your dreams for whatever reason. Well, now is the time to choose yourself, dream again and become more.

Renew Your Mindset

As I earlier wrote, making a U-turn first requires a mental transformation. This is achievable by engaging in daily little good-new-habits that changes your thinking over time. Here are some;

- Invest in yourself daily- self-care, self-motivation,

self-growth. Prioritize yourself.

- ☐ Make room for learning-listen to intelligent podcasts, read enlightening books, and get engaged with business news and updates. Grow intellectually.

- Get creative- get new skills and exhibit them,

hone old skills and explore old talents. Live every day with something to look back to.

Get Out There

For us women, some spaces are a restriction, whether

boldly spelled out or silently communicated. This should

not in any way deter you from embarking on your life's course. Instead, it should stir you up to go in headstrong.

The following are ways to break the embargo;

- Know your onions; be grounded in whatever field you decide to go

- into. Know virtually everything related to your chosen area of work. This will give you the confidence needed to get into the room and contribute your quota as a credible member.

- Grab your coat; occupy your deserved position- be it managerial or

organizational- with total confidence and being grounded. After doing away with mediocrity, you will realize you deserve a seat at the table, a stage, a business, or an enterprise.

Always remember, that your dreams are valid.

CONCLUSION

With the initial facts stated in this book, gender equality can only be attained by eliminating gender stereotypes that harm women's lives.

This is not a rebellion, but a rebirth. It's about putting the appropriate people and things

in place, regardless of gender or unfounded myths, so that we can achieve greatness in the world and, most importantly, a happier life.

Do not let stereotypes define you; define yourself instead. Never cave in, be resilient!

You will ultimately succeed if you decide to use your full potential on the planet starting right away!

www.ingramcontent.com/pod-product-compliance
Lightning Source LLC
LaVergne TN
LVHW020545160826
845677LV00015B/4217

* 9 7 9 8 3 6 2 5 2 1 2 6 4 *

www.ingramcontent.com/pod-product-compliance
Lightning Source LLC
LaVergne TN
LVHW020545160826
845677LV00015B/4212

* 9 7 9 8 8 4 6 3 3 5 2 0 2 *